Two miles north of Hell, a deadbeat narrator spots Satan
filling up his red Corvette at the 7-Eleven. Satan's a
washed-up has-been who's totally lost his edge . . . until
he falls in love with our narrator and the two embark on
a torrid romance, by turns screwball, surreal, terrifying
and tender.

'*Christopher Brett Bailey is a spectacularly brilliant
wordsmith . . . his brain is permanently on fire. Hop on
the back of his Harley, hold tight, you won't regret it.*'

Terry Gilliam

I Saw Satan at the 7-Eleven

Christopher Brett Bailey is a writer, performer and musician. He is a Cancer with a Leo Rising and has a bowling average of 149. He grew up on the US/Canada border and now lives in London with two cats and his much, much better half.

CHRISTOPHER BRETT BAILEY

I Saw Satan at the 7-Eleven

faber

First published in 2026
by Faber and Faber Limited
The Bindery, 51 Hatton Garden
London, EC1N 8HN

Typeset by Brighton Gray
Printed and bound in the UK by CPI Group (Ltd), Croydon CRO 4YY

A CIP record for this book
is available from the British Library

ISBN 978–0–571–40582–4

Printed and bound in the UK on FSC® certified paper in line with our continuing
commitment to ethical business practices, sustainability and the environment.
For further information see faber.co.uk/environmental-policy

Our authorised representative in the EU for product safety is
asy Access System Europe, Mustamäe tee 50, 10621 Tallinn, Estoni
gpsr.requests@easproject.com

2 4 6 8 10 9 7 5 3 1

I Saw Satan at the 7-Eleven premiered at Soho Theatre, London, on 21 April 2026, with the following creative team:

Writer & Performer Christopher Brett Bailey

Producer Beckie Darlington
Lighting Designer Alex Fernandes
Outside Eyes Rens Tesink, Felicia Kaspar and Max Elton

I Saw Satan at the 7-Eleven was seed commissioned by Fremantle and English Touring Theatre for *That Podcast*.

This stage version is adapted from the novella of the same name, published by Spender Books in 2023. Many thanks to George Spender.

I SAW SATAN AT THE 7-ELEVEN

CHAPTER ONE

I was born in a one-horse town. Two miles north of Hell.

Nothing much ever happened . . .

Except for this one thing . . .

I saw Satan at a 7-Eleven one time. He was dressing low-profile, but it was definitely him: red skin, horns, barbed tail, cloven hoofs, black goatee. He was unmistakable. Satan was buying soy milk and forty bucks' worth of unleaded fuel.

'Which pump sir?' said the clerk.

'Pump six,' said Satan, obviously.

The clerk looked up from his jerk-off magazine and started whimpering and sighing and sobbing and crying and pissing at the same time – liquid shooting from his tear ducts and his dick hole like a water feature. Satan took this as an indication that his gas was on the house. Satan tossed a coin onto the counter for the soy milk, the coin was red-hot and glowing. My mouth fell open and I dropped the toilet paper and eggs I was carrying.

Outside in the parking lot, Satan was polishing his windshield. Satan drove a Corvette, obviously. I went outside, kept my distance, eyeballed him wiping dead bugs from his wing mirrors. Then he struck a rebel pose with one foot up on the bumper like James Dean and he called out, 'I'm not a hippie. I'm lactose intolerant.'

'What?' I said . . . to Satan, 'Are you talking to me?'

'I saw you eyeing up my soy milk and I want to set the record straight. I'm. No. Hippie.'

I smiled. Which seemed to tick him off. 'Do you even know who I am?'

'Yes,' I said, 'I, I, uhh, think I do. Yes.'

'Think? You think? I'm one of the two most powerful beings in this universe! And you *think?*'

I looked at his greying beard, his receding hairline, and I thought, 'Sure – okay, buddy, maybe you *used* to be all-powerful but these days?'

Satan glared, offended, like he could read my thoughts. He growled in a tar-black voice, 'Get. In.'

I thought about my options. Weighed up all the pros. Weighed up all the cons.

He beckoned me forward with a big red claw.

I got in the car.

We sat for several minutes in an awkward silence, Satan revving the engine, doing breathing exercises. Breathing in, breathing out, breathing in, breathing out.

'I'm not a hippie, okay? . . . I have respiratory issues.'

'Satan, I'm starting to get the impression that you've lost your edge.'

Indignant, his nostrils flared and he put his pedal to the floor. We tore out of the gas station, tires screaming. He ran a hundred red lights in a row and swerved in order to hit an old woman who was crossing the road, the grille of the Corvette sliced her in two, her dentures flew up into the air and the windshield wipers squeaked as segments of her face smeared against the glass.

'Jeez! You don't stop for red lights, huh?'

'I don't stop for anything,' Satan cracked a beer and loaded a crackpipe and shifted gears and greased his pompadour. All at the same time. 'But I expecially, I expecially don't stop for red lights. Red don't mean stop to the Devil. Look at my skin? Would you associate the colour red with the words *no, stop, slow down*, if you were born red?'

Satan explains that stop signs and stop lights being red is an anti-communist plot, an anti-Native American plot too. Satan, it turns out, is a communist. Satan, it turns out, is part Cherokee.

The engine beats like a petrol heart, gasoline flows through it like blood, pistons pump like Dave Lombardo, tires squeal like pinch harmonics.

'Think about it . . . Red doesn't mean stop . . . it means GO!: red lipstick, red-light district, red embers on the lit tip of a cigarette,' Satan huffs his crackpipe, 'GO!' He pounds on the dashboard with cloven fists. 'Your brain knows it, your heart knows it, your loins know it.'

I look over at Satan's lap and see that his jeans are now full. The Devil is DTF, obviously.

I ask Satan to please pull over for me to piss.

He says, 'That's what windows are for,' and motions for me to unbuckle.

Just as I am unbuckling and standing up on the seat, to piss out the window into the rushing wind, Satan pulls a lever, and the convertible top goes down.

We hit a speed bump and I bounce up out of the car and get tangled in the electrical wires above. (Like a low-flying bird in a recurring dream, a bird which probably represents freedom or self-actualisation, which in some languages are the same word.)

I am gently electrocuted by the power lines I am tangled in. It is not unpleasant. A weaker man would have given up the ghost and become an angel, but I've got the constitution for electrocution and am drawn to power in all its forms.

Satan points and laughs and lets me sizzle. A bird waddles over, starts pecking at my freckles, mistaking them for seeds.

'Ow,' I giggle 'cause it tickles, 'Satan, look at this bird!'

Satan reverses his car into the post, the wood splinters and falls like chopped lumber. I come crashing down.

'That's not a bird. That's a camera with wings. Get away from it,' and Satan plucks all of the feathers off to prove it is a camera. It squawks in agony the whole time, to prove it is a bird.

Satan says, 'If you're a bird . . . fly away,' and launches it into the air.

The bird cannot fly because it does not have any feathers so it just kind of . . . falls onto the ground, and writhes. Now, I don't have a stomach for cruelty against animals, so I choose to believe that Satan is right, that that thing writhing in agony is probably just a camera. I feel the urge to cry but think I probably shouldn't.

We drive a few more miles, me sulking.

Satan says, 'You're sulking.'

I say, 'I'm not sulking.'

Satan says, 'You wanna hear music? We'll hear music,' and opens his glove compartment. He has a vast collection of cassette tapes: death metal, thrash metal, speed metal, sleaze metal, sludge metal, doom metal, drone metal, hair metal, nu metal, old metal, proto metal, power metal, industrial metal, first wave – second wave – third wave – fourth wave black metal, white metal, new wave of British heavy metal, new wave of traditional . . . , funeral doom, death doom, melodic death doom, AOR, hard rock and progressive rock with metallic tendencies . . . plus rockabilly, gangsta rap, dubstep, country-western, and a compilation of classical music pieces all deploying the tritone, the Devil's interval. Satan's music taste is post-genre, obviously.

All the tapes play backwards, of course, making psychedelic sucking sounds like *thhp thhp thhp thhp thhp thhp*.

This goes on for an hour. Satan sings along. He knows all the choruses in reverse. 'I can't get no satisfaction' backwards becomes 'on on on, noitcafsitas on teg t'nac I' and 'stand by your man' becomes 'nam rouy yb dnats'.

Eventually I switch the tape deck off. 'Can we just listen to the dang radio?'

'The dang radio? The radio is nothing but jingles and sloganeering and mind control and prank phone calls.'

I say, 'Yeah. And music.'

'Yeah. And music. Look kid, if you've got something to say . . . why don't you just go ahead and say it?'

I want to tell him to go to Hell. Instead, I just say, you know, I just say . . . 'Go home.'

'Fine,' Satan says, 'we'll listen to the dang radio.' And he reaches under his seat and pulls out a tinfoil hat. It is a Stetson. It is a tinfoil Stetson hat. He pulls it on over his horns.

'Where's yours?' he says.

'My what?'

'Your tinfoil hat.'

'I don't have one.'

'The AM/FM receiver goes both ways! Don't you know that? The radio won't be transmitting my deepest darkest thoughts to the whole world.'

'Whatever, man.'

'And if you die of brain cancer? I won't be coming to your funeral,' Satan says, tipping his tinfoil Stetson hat and turning the radio on.

The radio says, '–ay tuned to this station for your chance to win five hundred –'

KEEOW, I switch it off. 'You're right, the radio is crapola.'

'Atta boy,' Satan says, 'let's celebrate.'

In order to celebrate? He swerves and runs over a pair of hitchhikers.

We get out to check that they are dead.

They are.

Satan says, 'I hope the police get here soon, I love having my mugshot taken.'

The police don't come. So, Satan sets off an emergency flare hoping it will attract the authorities. It doesn't.

We wait around for an hour or so 'cause Satan wants to take credit. He wants the world to know: these dead hitchhikers are his doing. Satan uses his backup emergency flare to set his car on fire, in the hopes that the burning automobile will attract the police. It doesn't.

We scream into the starry night, 'Police! Police! Come and get us!'

. . . Nothing.

So, we decide to thumb a ride to the nearest police station, to confess. We stand on the shoulder of the road, waiting for destiny to slow down and pick us up. It starts to rain. So, Satan rips off the brim of his Stetson hat and fashions me a tinfoil beret. And for the first time ever I feel completely sure my brain is safe. That my deepest, darkest thoughts are not being broadcast to the whole world.

CHAPTER TWO

We wait for an hour. No cars come. We walk. Ten miles in the rain. We are drenched, sodden, waterlogged by the time we hit the edge of town. I march Satan to the police station.

Outside, we see a long line of people coming down the steps, wrapping round the building, stretching up the block.

We join the end of the line, ask the chump in front of us, 'Hey what's going on?'

'Well, we're all here to confess crimes. I'm here 'cause I stabbed my daughter in the face with a fork. She didn't even do nothin' to provoke me. I was just in that kind of a mood.'

'Jeez,' whispers Satan, wiping rain from his face, 'there must be four hundred people in this line. There sure is a lot of crime in this town, huh?'

'Sure is. Hell is only two miles that way,' the kid-stabber gestures south. 'Evil wafts across the border. Like how they got good Mexican food in Arizona? We got a lotta evil here.'

Now, I can tell by the way he says this that the kid-stabber does not recognise Satan. None of these people do. It's dark, it's raining, he has his tinfoil Stetson on, and he is decades past his prime.

Satan clutches my arm, we storm up the block towards the police station, passing pederasts and pickpockets and petty thieves and prostitutes and perjurers and villains of every description. Satan 'excuse me, pardon me, excuse me, pardon me's' his way to the front of the line, approaches the rookie cop who mans the clipboard.

'How long is the wait to get in there and confess?'

'Current wait time is nine hours, forty-eight minutes.'

Satan sneers.

'Come on, buddy. We're understaffed. You know how it is.'

'What about if it's a really bad crime?'

'What crime is it?'

Satan puffs his chest out: 'Double. Homicide.'

'Nah . . . get to the back of the line.' He shoos Satan with his clipboard.

'Do you even know who I am? I'm the Devil . . . THE . . . DEVIL . . . ! ! !'

The cop rolls his eyes, 'Sure you are, buddy.'

Satan turns beet-red with embarrassment, not that you can tell. I can tell . . . that Satan is crestfallen. He is a crestfallen angel.

So, we link arms and walk round the corner, strolling past the clock tower, cross the town square where the hobos are peeing on each other, through the botanical gardens to the graveyard at the back of the cathedral. Satan sneers at the steeple. The steeple wilts.

At the front of the cathedral there is another long line, this one full of sinners, thousands of people desperate to get in there and confess to a priest . . . to tell all about their affairs and molestations and their homicidal fantasies and their laziness and their greed and their unquenchable desire to kidnap their neighbour and cut each of her digits off one-by-one and feed them to her. And how terrified they are of their own minds, even though they know they'd never have the balls to do something like that, with questions on their lips like am I a bad person and can you go to Hell for just thinking about that stuff?

Some religious zealots in line nudge each other and whisper. One of them has recognised Satan. They boo him and give him the thumbs down, call him a has-been. Satan runs into the graveyard, sits on a tombstone, does breathing exercises. He brings some Rescue Remedy out his pocket and drops two drops onto his forked tongue. One drop on each fork.

I want to tell Satan that I accept him. Even in his worn-out condition. Instead I say, 'Come on Satan . . . I'll buy you a beer.'

The nearest bar is the Gumdrop Tavern. A joint as sticky as it sounds.

Satan says, 'Beer is for children. Let me do the ordering,' and orders us each a shot of penicillin. We knock those back. He orders us each a tumbler full of neat carbon monoxide, 'the finest intoxication money can buy'.

I clock the prices on the chalkboard and say, 'Wow Satan that's pretty generous. Are you sure?'

Satan is a gazillionaire, obviously.

We take a corner booth.

The bartender brings us water to sip between glugs of poison.

'I don't drink water,' Satan says. 'Water has chemicals in it that change the way you vote.'

A song comes on the jukebox, a hit that we all know and love, whatever song you're imagining? That's the song it was.

I ask Satan if he'd like to dance. Satan tells me he thinks he's dyspraxic. So we make conversation, do the verbal dance. And Satan is, in his way, quite charming. He certainly has a lot of opinions:

'Elvis is still alive, Paul McCartney is dead, whoever killed Kennedy isn't who they said. Lee Harvey Oswald couldn't pass a lie detector test to prove he didn't pull the trigger 'cause he couldn't remember not pulling it.'

'Why not?'

'They wiped his memory. And as the altar boy said to the bishop who was cornholing him at the time . . . wipe my ass if you must but don't you dare wipe my memory.'

I take a swallow of carbon monoxide and I say, 'Ach this conspiracy stuff, man, you know what I think? I think the real conspiracy would be if everything *was* exactly as it seems.'

Satan looks wounded. Gets up. Goes to the bathroom, pisses on the toilet seat, doesn't flush, doesn't wash his hands. Comes back to our table, asks me what I think of the election.

'What election?'

'Any election.'

'I don't vote.'

Satan is disgusted that I would let my constitutional right swill down the plughole like that. Tells me I have to vote.

I say, 'Okay, supposing next time I do vote, who should I vote for?' He tells me I oughta vote the way he votes.

I ask him how he votes. He tells me. And it's no surprise, Satan votes the opposite to you. Obviously.

Another round of carbon monoxide arrives. Satan takes a big swig, swills it around his mouth, shafts of light shine out through his pores.

'I give people their power. Politicians, celebrities, warlords, if you've heard of somebody chances are I had a hand in it.' He looks around the bar, points at some old movie posters on the wall, 'I introduced James Dean to hair gel, taught Humphrey Bogart to smoke, and I gave that peroxide hairdo to Marilyn Monroe.

'But I didn't only do good things for culture. I bought the bullet for Mark David Chapman which killed John Lennon. I said to Janis Joplin, "How about just one more drink?"'

'I guess you snuffed the good guys too, right? You killed Gandhi and Martin Luther King?'

'Nope. US government took care of that. But I helped Doctor King out of a tough spot.'

'How so?'

'Gave him writing advice. Told him writing is editing. You gotta cut the crap and get to the point. See, I visited Martin Luther King in August of '63. He was pacing round the typewriter, drafting his "I Have a Dream" speech. And he was nervous as heck, 'cause it was the night before the big day. You wanna know what the first draft of that fuckin' speech was?'

I nod.

'"*I have dinner and then I have ice cream, I drink rye whiskey, I take an antacid 'cause I got this heartburn thing, then I lay down on the bed and I don't always drift off right away, sometimes I have to count sheep, other times I take a sleeping pill, anyhow one way or another I generally get to the land of nod about thirty minutes after my head hits the pillow and when it does: I have a dream . . .*"

'So, Doctor King read me this and I said, "Uhh, Martin, can I make a suggestion? You're gonna be talking to thousands of people, your voice will ricochet off buildings, my man. So you wanna edit it down to just the punchiest couple words. I'm thinking, why not start with . . . 'I have a dream'."

'. . . And Martin said, "Don't you think they wanna know about my antacid, you know, my heartburn?" and I said, "I don't think that's of the utmost, Doctor King. All due respect" . . . And he went silent and thought about it, "I'll see how I feel tomorrow, once I'm in situ."'

'Satan, I cannot believe that you would help out a good guy.'

Satan says, 'No such thing as a good guy. No such thing as a bad guy either. Life ain't like that.'

Satan winks. I think about what he's saying. No such thing as good people. Or bad people. Maybe it's the candlelight or maybe it's the booze, maybe it's the jingle on the jukebox but there is tension between us now. Tension of a carnal nature.

Satan stares at me like a dog stares at an empty food bowl. He says, 'So. How about it?'

'Mmm . . . I got a headache.'

Satan looks hurt. He sulks to the bathroom, takes a shit on the toilet seat, doesn't wipe or wash his hands. He comes back, says, 'I don't need you to have fun. I'm gonna have a threesome.'

'A threesome?'

'Yeah, I'm gonna find the oldest person in this Gumdrop Tavern and the youngest. And I'm gonna fuck 'em both. Just to prove I still got it. To prove it to you, the world, and anyone else who cares to watch.'

Satan does a lap of the Gumdrop Tavern, hunting his prey. He finds the youngest right away, up by the movie posters . . . It's a cardboard cut-out of Shirley Temple. He plonks her down on the pool table. Chats her up. Then he spots the oldest: a skeleton nailed to the tavern wall.

He rips it down. The skeleton's been dead for a century. Shirley Temple doesn't look a day over eight. Satan and the skeleton and the cardboard cut-out have a threesome on the pool table. Satan staring at me the entire time, thrusting, caressing, nibbling, chewing. Satan runs his hand through Shirley's curls and penetrates the eye sockets of the skeleton, staring at me, unblinking.

After an hour of this I lick my lips and wink. Satan cums. A five-foot flame shoots out of his sex, cremating the skeleton, singeing all the hair off Shirley Temple's head. She shrieks and runs out of the bar.

Back at our table, Satan pulls out from his shirt a necklace. He rips it off his neck and dangles it. It's an upside-down crucifix, rusty and ancient. He stuffs it into my hand.

'What's this?'

'I like you, okay?'

'So?'

'Something to remember me by.'

Now, I could tell he liked me. If you wanna know the truth and this is the truth: Almost nobody falls in love with me but the people who do tend to fall pretty hard.

'So . . .' Satan says, 'How about it?'

'I told you once already . . . I got a headache.'

'But you have to put out! I just gave you my necklace!'

Satan thinks he can buy affection with jewellery.
Obviously.

Offended, he storms outside. I follow. He smokes and
broods in the parking lot, hopes that somebody will
recognise him and ask for an autograph. They don't.
I should probably go home but instead I start slashing
car tires with a switchblade. I have no idea why I did this,
to impress him, I guess? Next thing, even though I don't
really want to, Satan and I have an awkward kiss . . .
against a dumpster.

He tells me how invigorated he feels, 'so full of vim'. He
pops a power boner, and propositions me.

'Satan I am not going to *do* you up against this dumpster.
Or anywhere else al fresco.'

'Fine. We'll go to your house.'

I picture that. I have to tell him the truth: 'Satan . . . I live
with my parents . . .'

'So?'

'You are not rutting me in my childhood bed!'

'Is there a hotel in this dogshit town? Money is no object.'

I picture the two hotels in our town. The crummy, run-down, flea-pit one that nobody ever goes to. And the upscale one with a rooftop pool and Michelin-star bistro.

We walk to the wrong side of the tracks, down the decommissioned railway line to the industrial warehouses, past crackheads and cracks in the sidewalk, we squeeze down a network of narrow alleys and come out by the old bingo hall that is currently squatted by an arms dealer, past the vaudeville theatre that shows stag reels of snuff porn, past the barbershop where the rats get their fur shaved short, and we finally arrive at the tar-black brickwork of the crummy, run-down, flea-pit hotel.

'One dollar per night,' boasts the blinking neon sign out front.

'One dollar per night?' Satan says, 'What kind of a room can you get for one dollar?'

CHAPTER THREE

The hotel room is the size of a cigar box. In there is brown peeling everything – wallpaper, rug, floorboards, bed sheets crusted with faeces from the last guys.

Satan locks the door and flicks the light. The bulb fritzes on and off in time with the vibrations and choo-chooing of railroad tracks outside the window. Satan comes and stands behind me, pressing his weight into me, his belly heaving into my back. He licks the back of my neck. In two spots because his tongue is forked.

We slow-dance to the rattling of the windowpane and the grinding of locomotive gears. And Satan is, for a brief moment, a gentleman. He curtsies at the end of our waltz.

He yanks the shit-spattered duvet off the bed and fashions a yoga mat on the floor. He does jaguar pose . . . pyramid pose . . . downward-facing dingus –

'I'm not some yoga freak, okay? I got problems with my hamstrings.'

– cobra pose . . . shirshasana . . . shoulder stand with lotus legs.

He rolls back up to standing: 'Okay. Enough foreplay. Take it off.'

'Take what off?'

'Everything.'

'Everything?'

'Even your socks.'

Satan, fully clothed, watches me sashay and pirouette and Chattanooga two-step around the room, pulling off one article of clothing after another, dropping them onto the floor.

For a moment I feel empowered. Then a toilet flushes above us, and I feel self-conscious . . . about my varicose veins, my high forehead, my powder-white A-cup moobs. I stop undulating.

'Why did you stop undulating?'

'Well . . . I just . . . I guess . . . I . . .'

Cool air mottles my flesh. I feel young. I feel inexperienced. I feel teenaged: I sprout a pimple and the pimple pops.

'Would baby feel more comfortable if both of us boys were in the buff?'

I don't answer.

Satan unbuttons his shirt, nipples poke out of his flesh like arrowheads in the dirt of an archaeological dig. I can see his jeans cage a python, dribbling damp, pre-cum darkening the denim.

I want to say something, anything, but the words won't come. I open my mouth and it's just

'. . . . .'

'cause the thing I am desperate to say I cannot. I am paralysed by . . . what? Fear? Excitement? Trepidation? Perhaps a perplexing triplet of the three.

Satan peels off his last article of clothing: a G-string made of human flesh. And there before me the great beast stands naked. Wings like tattered sails on an old warship. Nipple ring the size of a door knocker on a medieval castle door. A thirty-gallon beer gut scarred from hellfire. Floorboards creak as Satan totters towards me. He backs me against the grandfather clock, says, 'Let's compare ding-dongs.'

Satan takes mine in one hand. And his in the other. There is nothing erotic about the hold, he holds it like a doctor would. Makes eye contact with me, it's the most intense soul-gaze of my life. His pupils swirl like marbles melting in the molten heat of Mars. Our temperatures rise and we both get wood. My wood is a splinter compared to Satan's. His wood is a rough-barked log dripping ash and hot embers. It grows and grows until it's the size of a canoe. It has to bend in two places just to fit in this tiny hotel room.

Mine is still a splinter.

Satan kisses me. Hard, like he's eating an apple. 'Please . . . I just . . .' I say, pulling away, smashing my head on the grandfather clock.

Satan throws me down onto the bed. He tries to force himself inside. But I am not prepared. Things are too dry back there. I say, 'Satan . . . please . . . please . . . slow down . . . I need to be romanced.'

He doesn't hear me because he's wriggling and writhing and roaring and sighing.

'Satan! Satan! Please! Stop!'

'Yeah? Yeah?' he grunts, lightning bolts shoot from his eye sockets, eyeballs spin like jackpot jackpot jackpot.

'Don't! . . . Stop!' I scream.

'Don't stop? I won't stop! I promise I won't stop!'

'No! I don't want this! I changed my mind!' But Satan is inside of me, filling me up with all of him. I grasp a hand out and fumble the telephone off the bedside table and clobber it down on Satan's head. The bell mechanism ring-a-lings as Satan slurps out of me and falls backward. I scramble to the bathroom. Slam the door shut. Satan, panting, still aroused, his voice muffled by the door, 'What? . . . What just happened?'

My brain goes, 'ohmygod ohmygod ohmygod ohmygod ohmygod ohmygod', my legs tremble, my ass roars in pain.

Satan's cloven hooves click-clack the floorboards as he approaches the bathroom door. Knocks politely.

I don't answer.

He knocks again.

'Go away!' . . . I experience my own voice like it's someone else's on the radio. It sounds more confident than I feel.

Satan clip-clops away. The bedsprings boing as he sits down. 'Did I do something wrong?'

I explain to Satan that I said 'No' . . . and he didn't listen . . . that I can say No at any time. And he has to honour that.

'Any time?'

'Any time,' I say. 'Before the act. Or during the act, if I say stop, you have to.'

'Have to *what* exactly?'

'Stop!'

'Well . . . that's not how it works in Hell.'

I open the bathroom door. Satan is lying in bed, facing
the wall. Tail twitching in agitation. I've wounded his ego.
Satan's self-image is ornate and like all things that are
ornate it is fragile. I tiptoe to my clothing, start pulling it on.

'Where are you going?'

'Out.'

'For?'

'A walk.'

'Where to?'

'Nowhere.'

Satan grunts. I turn the light switch off. The room goes
dark except for a red glow that emanates from Satan's
crotch. It intensifies as a hot ember from his penis sets the
bed sheet alight. He doesn't even flinch, just scratches at
these flames like you scratch at your pubic lice.

'Will you be here when I get back?'

'Yeah.'

'Promise?'

Satan rolls over and starts snoring. It's the loudest thing
I've ever heard. It shakes the whole hotel. Out in the
corridor there is a mirror rattling on the wall because of
Satan's snoring. And as I pass I see my reflection shatter.

CHAPTER FOUR

Outside, rats fuck in gutters but otherwise it's quiet.
I walk ten blocks through swirling toxic haze clouds of
pollution and don't see another person. I walk on shaky
legs, ass sore, doing breathing exercises to calm my
jangled nerves. Breathing exercises? God, I'm becoming
just like him.

I pass empty storefront after empty storefront after empty
storefront after empty storefront, my reflection flickering
in derelict windows.

A bar materialises. The bouncer says, 'Heey, it's singles'
night.'

I go in and sit up at the bar. The place is called Hula-Hula.
And it's the only joint I know about open this late.
The decor is Hawaii-Disco. Everything is a mirror or a
coconut or a pink sunset or a surfboard or a crashing
wave or a fibreglass dance floor that lights up when you
shimmy across it. A waitress boogies past and lassoes my
neck with a necklace of flower petals.

The dance floor is empty. The tables are crammed full of
lonely singles, all too nervous to talk to one another. Or

too sad. Or too ugly. The cardboard cut-out of Shirley
Temple is there. She's drowning her sorrows at a corner
table by an arcade machine. She sits alone. I notice her.
Hope she doesn't notice me, avert eye contact. Too late.

'Hey . . . you . . . you . . . hey . . . hey . . . hey . . . you . . .
mister . . . hey . . . hey . . . mister . . . you . . . hey . . .'
comes her high-pitched child voice, with a timbre like
scrunching paper or a cardboard box collapsing, 'Hey . . .
you . . . you . . . mister . . .' The words tumble from
her like a piano falling down a staircase, 'mIsTeR . . .
MisTer . . . yoU . . . YOu . . . HeY . . . yoUuuu . . .'

I look at her face. It's very unnerving 'cause though she is
sentient her facial expression is fixed, forever unchanging.

She climbs onto the bar stool next to mine, 'Barkeep!
Gimme another Black Widow.'

'What's a Black Widow?' I ask.

'Xanthan gum, squid ink, espresso, vodka, tequila, gin,
rye, Scotch, a twist of lime, a dusting of Scotch bonnet, in
a frosted glass with blow on the rim.'

'Blow? . . . You mean . . . ?'

The drink arrives and Shirley does a circular line off the
rim of the glass. 'Achhh, post-nasal drip!' she winces and
gets a nosebleed and washes the snot down her throat
with a mouthful of this concoction.

I order a lite beer.

Shirley says, 'Screw that, bring him something strong and European.'

The beer arrives. The bartender warns me it's 68% alcohol. I sip nervously. It tastes like Viking sweat.

Shirley asks me why I'm alone on singles' night, says a guy with my looks shouldn't be flying solo. I shift around awkwardly on my stool. I've never known how to take a compliment. Especially from older women. Or children. And Shirley Temple is both.

I stare at the charring down her edge, from where Satan came a flame and she caught fire. It looks painful and I'm dying to ask about it. I don't want to be rude, but I have to say something, so I say, 'You know back at the Gumdrop Tavern, earlier tonight . . .'

'Tonight?'

'Yeah, tonight.'

'What about tonight?'

'Earlier on . . . at the Gumdrop Tavern . . .'

'Wait. What's this about the Gumdrop Tavern?'

'Well, you were there earlier tonight . . .'

She says 'I know that, I'm me!'

I take a gulp of my beer. The 68% immediately fogs my everything. 'Uhh . . . Where was I?'

'When?'

'Just now. I mean *what* was I saying?'

'Saying about what?'

'Well exactly . . . *Where* was I?'

'I don't know where *you* were, but I was at the Gumdrop Tavern.'

'Oh yeah,' I say, remembering that I'd brought that up. 'I was *there* too, and I *saw* . . .'

'Saw what?'

'You know . . .'

'Oh. You mean, you saw what happened between me and that cranberry-red biker-looking fella? What a grade-A lummox he was! I'm minding my own business, he comes over and sweet-talks me, real candy, says what a fan he is of my screen work. Says, "Macaulay Culkin ain't got shit on you, you'll always be the grand empress of child stars." Then bends me over the snooker table, offers me twenty bucks if I'll jack him, I say, "Save your money, if the compliments keep coming, I'll jack you for free. Pro boner." But then he says he wants to make it a manage-a-trois and I don't speak French-fry, so I say, "What's that?" and he introduces me to this skeleton. Now necrophilia is not my thing so I say "No!" and try to squirm away but before I know it, he's unbuttoned and thrusting, and the skeleton has a bony hand on me . . .' Shirley pauses, takes a swig, 'Anyways, you'll never guess what happened next . . .'

I say, 'He ejaculated a flame out of his ding-a-ling. You caught fire and ran out into the rain.'

'Exactly! How did you know that?'

'Shirley, I was there.'

'Really?'

'That's how we got on to this conversation. I brought it up.' I hiccough. It smells like a tiny brewery has opened for business in my throat.

'Oh yeah . . .' Shirley drinks, then thinks, so hard she nearly falls off her stool, 'Why were you there?'

'I was there with him, kind of.'

'With, as in, like, on a . . . *date*?'

. . . So I tell her the whole story.

Everything.

Right from the beginning.

From, you know, when I went to the 7-Eleven. Just like I told you. Except this time, I'm careful to omit any parts that make me sound bad, and I ramp up all the parts that make Satan sound bad.

'Wow, that's a humdinger of a day,' Shirley says.

And just then we hear . . . short sharp intakes of breath all around the bar.

The doors of the Hula-Hula have swung open, there is a gun barrel pointing in from the street. It doesn't seem to be trained on anyone in particular, just generally menacing the nightclub.

The DJ cuts the music. We hear a blood-curdling scream.

The gun spits slugs from its tight metal mouth like, *rat-a-tat-rat-a-tat-rat-a-tat-tat*. Those sober enough to duck the bullets, do. The rest get filled with holes. I survived on account of Shirley. She yanked me down and made a barrier out of bar stool for us both. It if wasn't for her I'd be human Swiss cheese.

The gunshots stop. We hear the impotent *clack-clack-clack* of the empty chamber. The nightclub doors swing shut, and we hear footsteps running away. The DJ puts the music back on. The waitress boogies round the room putting the deceased into body bags. The bartender offers the survivors a free round on the house. I decline on account of I'm drunk enough to see triple, thanks to those strong European beers I've been glugging.

'How can I ever repay you?'

'For what?'

'Saving my life?' I reach into my pocket for money and all I find is the necklace Satan gave me. I offer that.

'I have a sponsorship with Dior. I have no need of that hunk-a-junk.'

Shirley's complimentary Black Widow arrives. The clock on the wall claims it's five-thirty in the morning. The sun rising out the window corroborates this.

'Well, I gotta be going.' I say.

'So soon?'

'Maybe see you around.'

Shirley snorts the line off the rim of her glass . . . 'I'd like that.'

I pour myself out of the nightclub and walk the neighbourhood. Ankles soft from alcohol. Rats have tender morning sex in gutters. I am heartened to see them deploying dental dams and condoms because, do you have any idea how dirty a rat is? I see a rat couple change positions from 69 to 70, working their way through the Kama Sutra.

Besides this carnal commotion it's quiet out. I pass the demolition derby track and the long-ago-melted ice rink, cut down a side street towards the cathedral. There, I see Satan's face over and over and over. Not his actual face. Black-and-white xeroxes of his mugshot are stapled to telephone poles, pinned under windshield wipers, and blowing around in the breeze. I pick one out of the air, my booze-addled vision can barely make sense of the words that are all swimming on the page. Some words swim backstroke, some swim breaststroke. There's a bunch that are doing synchronised swimming routines from old MGM musicals. I clear my throat passive-aggressively, and the words stop swimming. They stay still for a second, so I can read them . . .

```
ATTENTION EVERYBODY,

The DEVIL has been apprehended. Is in
POLICE custody. A TRIAL was held. Satan
was found GUILTY of every crime and
misdemeanour in the book, and several
that aren't in the book. He will be
fast-tracked to the electric chair. Our
town is HONOURED to be snuffing him.
That will really put us on the map,
eh? Anyway, SATAN is scheduled to be
EXECUTED today at 11 a.m., if you'd
like to observe that, don't be late.

                        - Sincerely yours,
                          THE AUTHORITIES.
```

I lay down fetal on the steps of the cathedral. The steeple stands so stiff, so tall, as if to mock Satan. I shake my fist at it. It gets hard and veiny and cums a rainbow of wafers, wine and fish. The church bells ring. A bird caws and swoops down to peck at holy wafers and I feel certain that bird is a camera.

CHAPTER FIVE

Outside the courthouse is a very a long line. Of goths, metalheads and headbangers, punks, witches, warlocks, and of course, actual Satanists. They have travelled from all over the country, nay, the world, to show their respects. To glimpse their idol in the flesh. To glimpse him in death. I join the back of this line, and am informed by a girl with King Diamond tattoos that the event sold out in seconds. Thankfully a scalper is working the line. I pay twice face value for a seat in row F.

The line starts moving up the sidewalk, sun glaring, all of us sweating in our denim and leather. We get to the bottom of the courthouse steps. Halfway up is a news crew. Cameras pointed at a defence attorney in a sharp suit, hair slicked back. 'Listen people, incarceration would be one thing. But our state's frankly draconian judicial system should not have a right to terminate this creature's life. The fact that this medieval practice still happens in our country but does not happen where my client comes from . . . literally Hell, should shake even the most hard-hearted among us to the core. Today, our nation hangs its head in shame.'

The line of Satanists erupts in applause. Counter-protesters boo and wave cardboard signs scrawled with holy scripture and anti-Devil propaganda.

Inside, vendors sell T-shirts and hot dogs and popcorn. The opening act is some small-time serial killer no one has ever heard of. When they pull the lever and fry this guy the audience barely stirs. As they cart his corpse away there's a smattering of polite applause. A voice says over the sound system, 'Three minutes till Satan's execution. Please take your seats,' and the lights dim. I put on the tinfoil beret because I want Satan to spot me in the crowd and see me wearing it.

A grizzled old cop steps up to the microphone. And he says 'Ladies and gentleman, we have a very special guest' and he introduces the Pope who has flown in from the Vatican and he ambles up onto the stage in his big stupid fucking hat and he unspools a scroll of paper longer than the River Nile. It's Satan's rap sheet – a list of offences stretching all the way back to the beginning of recorded history. The Pope reads the highlights, it takes an hour or two.

Then there's drum rolls and spotlights and they bring Satan out in chains. The orange of his prison jumpsuit clashes badly with the bright-red tone of his skin. It's a very unflattering colour combo under these stage lights. Satan gets dragged by prison guards and strapped into the electric chair.

A slow clap starts at the back of the hall.

Satan, suddenly aware of the size of the audience, can't believe his eyes. Thousands have made the pilgrimage. Outsiders of every stripe and subculture. Misfits and renegades to whom Satan is a symbol of rebellion. One by one, fists go up into the air and make devil horns. A sea of devil horns. Everyone does it . . . except for me. I am not there to worship him. I don't worship him. I am his equal.

Satan mugs for the crowd, swirling his forked tongue. The crowd roars in approval. My chest swells with pride. Satan suddenly spots me, he stops mugging, wells up, eyes filling with regret, he mouths, 'I'm sorry.'

I mouth, 'I forgive you.'

He mouths, 'I'm going to miss you.'

I open my mouth to mouth something, but I don't mouth anything because I'm not sure I will miss him. And I don't want to lie. Lying is not what mouths are for.

The house lights go down again, the grizzled old cop shushes the crowd. The audience stomps and chants, 'Sa-tan! Sa-tan! Sa-tan!' We are under the spell of his dark majesty, a force greater than law.

One witch at the back of the hall starts incanting Satanic verse. She's up on her feet convulsing uncontrollably, ripping her clothes off and smearing pigs' blood down her curves. A searchlight scans the crowd. A sniper takes her out. *THHHWP.* The audience hush down in their seats.

They shave Satan's head and fit him with electrodes. A tear comes to my eye. Satan screams in Latin. I have no idea what he's saying, and I doubt anybody else does either, 'cause we are an awful long way from Latvia.

They stuff Satan's screaming mouth with a ball gag. His last words and saliva slosh round the sides of it. They wet the top of his head with a sponge, and bring the metal cap down. They pull the elastic strap under his chin, snapping it real hard so it hurts.

You can hear a pin drop as they flip the switch. At first nothing happens . . . electricity courses through Satan but it seems to have no effect. If anything, it seems to energise him a tad, like a Nespresso. His eyes are looking provocatively *smug* for a guy who is riding lightning bareback.

One cop shrugs to another like, 'Well . . . what do we do?'

The other shrugs like, 'I guess we turn up the voltage.'

They turn the electricity higher . . . Satan doesn't flinch.

'Take the training wheels off!' screams the grizzled old-timer lighting one Marlboro off another.

'Really? We've never needed this much power to kill someone before.'

'Just do it! That's an order!' barks the lieutenant.

They crank the dial as far as it will go. Fifty thousand volts of power. Satan finally starts to flinch. Wriggles and writhes, face contorting in agony or ecstasy, it's hard to tell which.

'More!' barks the lieutenant.

'Yeah, more, fry this fucker!' chimes in the Pope.

They remove the limiter and crank the switch to maximum: a *googolplex* volts of power! Satan shrieks and sparks fly out of his mouth. His nipples get hard. His extremities flail as the electricity flows through him. We hear sizzling, fizzing, hissing. With a deafening snap his bones break apart, his arms and legs fly off, hurtling from the stage into the crowd. People dive and shove each other out of the way to catch his limbs like drumsticks thrown at a rock concert. They crank the power even higher. There's a violent flash like a firework, his horns get hard and spurt bone marrow, then melt like spent candles. The flesh of his face peels off revealing a mask of twitching muscle underneath, which flakes away, revealing his skeleton face. Eyeballs boil in their sockets, the rubber ball gag in his mouth liquifies, and the skeleton face appears to be grinning now, mocking the police. So, they push the electricity even further, so high the needle shoots out of the display panel into the eyeball of the Pope. They use so much electricity they blow the power grid, the entire country goes dark. But it does the trick . . .

Satan explodes. The electric chair is empty save for a
puddle of blood. Diabolical innards cling to the room like
confetti. But the Devil himself is gone.

There is a pause longer than most funerals.

Then the audience erupts into the *biggest* round of
applause of all time. It's like Glastonbury plus Woodstock
plus the Super Bowl plus New Year's Eve plus Gettysburg
plus Nuremberg plus the Sermon on the Mount
(I wasn't there, but I assume that was pretty loud) plus
the deafening applause from all my past performances
combined . . .

Sombre, we file out of the courthouse. Heads held low.

Outside, the night is full of ravens, a swarming black
mass cawing apocalyptic birdsong. They serenade the
Devil as his soul transfers to wherever you go to when
you're supposedly immortal, and then you die.

I look up, wondering how many of these birds are
cameras.

The crowd congregates. Black candles lit. Satanic hymns
sung. Tears, hugs, jubilation. For hours we refuse to leave
the courthouse steps, we camp there in protest.

Cops shout through megaphones, 'Go away! Loitering is
a crime! And we are tough on crime!'

We don't go.

They bring out tear gas and riot shields.

We go.

The crowd moves up Main Street, reminiscing about the historic event we just witnessed. Something to tell our grandkids about. Especially the part where Satan's eyeballs melted. The grandkids are gonna love that.

CHAPTER SIX

I say goodbye to my new friends, hug the girl with the King Diamond tats and we say, 'Let's keep in touch.' We both know we won't.

And what happened next . . .

. . . is almost *impossible* to explain . . .

. . . but I'll do my best . . .

The people all around – these metalheads and goths – step out of their black clothing. Tattoos disappear, skin turning back to virgin flesh. Nose rings disintegrate, piercing holes closing up.

The dark sky above us turns blue with wisps of bright yellow sunlight like hay. Ravens morph into blue jays and sing the C-major scale.

An ice-cream truck comes up the block handing out freebies. All the boarded-up shops in town become un-boarded and reopen for business.

In the alleyway where the heroin addicts are, addiction loses its grip and heroin turns to vitamin B inside of syringes.

Hunger turns to satisfaction.

And lies turn to truths in liars' mouths.

Ingrown toenails, bacterial vaginosis, arthritis, cancerous cells, precancerous cells – and whatever is ailing you – doesn't exist any more.

Cows break free of cages and roam free – not beef in waiting but animals once again – and critical levels of methane gas in the atmosphere are sucked back up cows' butts.

And above us we see the burns in the ozone layer repairing themselves.

Water – hitherto the most boring drink in the world – starts to taste like the life source it is. And beer, like a slow poison that bloats you.

Exercise, all of a sudden, became . . . possible. Push-ups and sit-ups, very easy. Sitting on your ass all day? Almost impossible.

Human looked upon human with sympathy and without suspicion.

In our town there was a woman whose entire existence since the beginning of time had been: hitting her husband in the head with a rolling pin. She paused and thought better of it.

A man who'd been kicking his mistress down a staircase
for eternity wound back to do so, then broke down
crying, begging forgiveness.

Murdered corpses reanimated at the morgue to tell
exactly what happened, to put the right killers behind
bars.

There was a radio station in our town that only played
free-form jazz. This wild angular music organised
itself into coherent linear melodies that everyone could
appreciate. All the minor chords turned to major chords.
Blues music just . . . ceased to exist.

The paintings of Jackson Pollock in the art gallery, threw
down their pretentions and reorganised their strokes into
figurative renderings people could understand: sunsets,
bowls of fruit, dogs playing pool.

The internet was un-invented, people's ability to
remember things for themselves came back, and to hear
each other, and to view each other with something –
anything – other than suspicion and derision and hatred
and hatred
and hatred
and hatred
and hatred . . .
became just a word.
A hypothetical that was fun to think about because it
didn't exist.

Like unicorns. Or alternate realities.
Just a fantasy that gave people pause.

The snake was exonerated
Once again just an animal
Phallic and scaly and whatnot
But just one of nature's creatures
Not carrying all this baggage
About, ya know, the fall of humanity.

Apples once again were just nature's toothbrush
A convenient food swinging from tree branches
No longer the weapon
That Eve used to fuck the world.

The world became . . . un-fucked.

Victims of Nigerian prince scams were reimbursed
And scammers the world over apologised to all their
victims
And to legitimate Nigerian princes
For the appropriation of their, uhhh, culture.

Layers of self-delusion flaked from the human
Filters fell from our lenses
Scales from our eyes
And we could look about the world without distortion
For the first time
And see
That it is a paradise
And see that it is

In fact, a picnic
And see
That it is good
Or at least
The best thing we've got.

The world is in fact, our oyster
And oysters
No longer caused diarrhoea and vomiting
Safe to eat no matter the month.

It was acknowledged that money is not only the root
Of all evil
But the branches and the leaves as well.

Neuroses disappeared, psychiatrists were out of a job,
asylums were empty.

Cain un-killed Abel
God un-flooded the world
Noah un-invented the Ark
The animals two-by-two – some of them were stuck in
unloving marriages – were permitted to divorce.

God breathed a huge sigh of relief.

Mother Nature iced her black eye . . . and prepared to be
un-harassed for the first time.

There was an End to War as sworn enemies fell in love
with each other and consummated on battle lines, sharing

resources, sharing information, sharing in the glory
of Creation.
As bombs sucked backwards up into airplanes
Flying back to the factories that made them
To get un-manufactured
And dollars evaporated from the bank accounts that
profit on mechanised death.

Pornography ceased to be the main way that people cum
And dating apps the main way they come together
And there was, as corny (and cheesy and naive and
unrealistic) as it sounds

There was LOVE

There was love

You could fucking FEEL IT

You could almost taste it or . . . what's the other sense?
I'm serious . . . it was like all five senses harmonically
vibrating or or or,
It was like an atmosphere that swirled around – I can't
explain it
I can't explain it
Except to say that it was

It was

Really really really . . . *really* . . . REALLY

Good.

I looked around and what did I see?
This festering wound of a world that we live in
Healing itself
Getting better
And better
Moving towards bliss
Perfection
And it was
it was . . .

Too good to last.

'What's going on down there?' God asked . . .

'Well, it's a world without Satan,' I said . . . 'This is what's
it's like when there's no evil in the world.'

'So there's no pain no agony no sadness no degradation
no compromise no deception no hatred et cetera?'

'Yeah,' I said.

'Without bad to resonate off of . . . good has no meaning.
People can't just be good because they're programmed to
be that way. They have to choose it . . .'

'Huh,' I said.

'That just how I see it,' God said, 'that isn't necessarily
how it is.'

And I realised then that the pocket of my jeans was
hot to the touch. Stuffed my hand in there, found the

upside-down crucifix on a chain, the necklace Satan gave
me in the bar? It was so hot I could barely hold it, the
metal glowing red.

I looked around at the world becoming beautiful and
thought, 'I guess I no longer need this . . .' but it was like
the necklace could read my thoughts. The necklace looked
as indignant as an inanimate object can look.

I tried to throw it away but it flew back into my hand
and growled, rolled over in my palm and showed me its
backside and there in tiny lettering was an inscription.
I squinted.

*Whoever is in possession of this necklace
at the time of Satan's expiration becomes
the new Satan. That's how immortality works.
A spirit is passed from living host to living host,
staying alive forever, like a virus.*

Under my breath I say, 'That's how immortality works?
Like *The Santa Clause* with Tim Allen? Satan is just like
a haunting that hopscotches like herpes across history?'
I look at the back of the necklace and the necklace
says . . .

Yes, that's how it works, you dickhead!

I catch my reflection and I can see now that my skin is turning from white to pink to red, my eyes are turning yellow, wings are sprouting, muscles are bulging from my clothes, I start to feel pretty warm from the inside but it's not the heat of a hot flash or a warm bath it's kind of like hellfire. I start to sweat in pools and gushes. Snake venom is alive inside of me. Snake venom is running through my veins instead of blood. I ache as the poison courses through me.

I catch my reflection again and the transformation is now complete. And I am completely unrecognisable.

'He's back!'
'He's risen from the dead!'
'Lucifer!'
'Beelzebub!'

A crowd forms with cellphones held high like pitchforks. Filming me for their vlogs and channels and Facebook Lives.

In the distance I hear sirens
Some narc has called the cops
The sounds of guns being loaded and engines turning over
The heat closing in
The heat coming
The crowd turns ugly
Pointing and screaming and baying for blood

So I do what anyone would do – I do what *You* would do.
I order . . . an Uber
To get me the heck outta Dodge
After a little bit of buffering I am connected to a driver
Iqbal – lovely chap – in a Toyota Prius
Registration ending 5KL

The Uber pulled out through an angry mob hollering
and pounding on the car like Beatlemania, except, you
know, they hate me. And then I realise, it's not *me* any
more . . .
I'm not me
The me I was is dead
This body that I am in will die
But the spirit who I am will live forever
It will only be mine for a short while
To carry like a baton.

The Uber leaves town, the town thins out to the suburbs
then to country roads. We pass the 7-Eleven, the
automechanics', the city dump, the baseball diamond, we
pass abandoned lot after abandoned lot after abandoned
lot. We arrive, finally, at the dead hitchhikers . . .
Their bodies are splayed, rotting, abuzz with flies. I scoop
these corpses up, drop them into the trunk of the Uber,
instruct Iqbal to take them to the police station. I say, 'I'll
give you five stars for this trouble,' and a big tip . . . and
I wave him off with cloven hand.

Satan's car – the Corvette – was where we'd left it . . .
I approach this burnt automobile.
And the necklace starts to throb . . . I pull the door
open, take a seat behind the wheel, and put the necklace
into the ignition. Just as I suspected: it fits. The crucifix
turns like a key. The engine roars. I put the Corvette in
reverse and back out onto the road. Point it due south.
Towards the border . . . towards my future, my destiny,
my kingdom, my safe haven. Two miles to Hell. I push
the accelerator. Vroom we Zoom, tires eat the road.
I switch the radio on, the sexless voice of the newscaster
'– several reported sightings today of, as incredible as this
sounds, the very beast that was exterminated yesterday.
Authorities are advising citizens to stay in their homes.
Once again, I repeat –' *KEEOW*. I turn the radio off.
I hear sirens from behind getting closer. I scream and
pound the dash. I push the accelerator to maximum,
the car hurtles forward, past the place where the world
becomes just dirt, I open up the glovebox and shove a
cassette tape in at random – my mouth screams along,
somehow magically knowing the words. Pedal floored,
one more mile to the border – WARNING – WARNING –
YOU ARE NOW LEAVING EARTH – the sirens wail,
gaining on me, they're right in my rear-view, cops and
army with rocket launchers and laser guns and a giant
fuckin' . . . like . . . net . . . thing. Machine-gun fire sprays,
a rocket screams from a launcher and explodes up ahead,
I swerve to miss the blast, downshift, correct the car,
upshift, step on it, through smoke and fire I drive. And the

dirt beneath my wheels and the sky above begin to crack
and splinter. The world that you and I know – the world
we live in – goes fuzzy and indistinct and fades out into
nothing. I push forward into the black, into a dark thick
mucus, the inky nowhere place, the void between worlds.
And up ahead in the distance is a giant blood-red orb . . .
like a sun made of molten lava. A throbbing blister about
to burst volcanic. I brace myself for impact and in a flash
of white light and psychedelic heat my car drives straight
into the heart of the thing, an exploding nuclear reactor,
drilling to the core of Mars, everything red, everything
crimson, everything blood, sticky and womb-like. The car
skids to a stop. I look in the rear-view and watch the skin
of this blister closing shut and sealing over . . . like it was
never punctured . . .

Like the world beyond it – this world you inhabit –
doesn't exist
Never did exist.
This world is nothing
And
I . . . am
Home.